NOBODY

Nobody + Opportunity = Somebody

BY RODNEY THOMAS

Charleston, SC
www.PalmettoPublishing.com

Nobody
Copyright © 2020 by Rodney L. Thomas

All rights reserved. This book or any portion thereof may not be reproduced or used in any manner whatsoever without the express written permission of the publisher except for the use of brief quotations in a book review.

Paperback ISBN: 978-1-64990-924-4

Special Dedication

For something special to happen, you need to be a special person and have special people around you regularly. Regular people cannot handle bright lights—only The Magnificent Seven! Seven brothers who did the unheard of in the city of lights:

Kenny O. T. Smith, Keven X, Destroy, Dice Smiles (RIP), Tone-P, Stick-Dun, Stim Diggah. Hip-hop will never be the same in the LV. Thank you for the ride. E-Slit (RIP), SCI-FY, Ty-Diggs, Sherita, and Ebony:

These people are a welcome mat for me, and I want to say thank you to The Welcome Mat!

Introduction

What is it to know who you are and what you are? A tough question to answer. Therefore, this book can help some people understand that it is not where you *start* but where you *finish*!

As you read, open your mind and confess who you may be.

Thank you for your time and blessing, because without you I cannot continue to *bless* others. Thank you Alfred, Joleen, Prime Events Staff and my little brother Twixx.

Enjoy the read, *Nobody:*
Nobody + Opportunity = Somebody.

The Beginning

Nobody + Opportunity = Somebody

Growing up in housing projects in Jersey City, New Jersey—the cousin of New York and referred to by many as the sixth borough—Rosie was ten years old when he envisioned his dream to have a company of his own. However, he felt that the dream was impossible to obtain because he was not a child born with a "silver spoon." He saw all the popular children given all the opportunities in all areas. Rosie felt that he was a nobody. Being in gym class proved he was a pretty good athlete, but because he was not popular, he was always picked last or not chosen at all. And to add insult to injury, he did not get to hang out with those considered to be the "kool kids" because he was a *nobody*.

Now, throughout the stories you will have to answer the question.

Rosie had friends at ten years old. He hung out with his certain type of friends. Some of his friends played hooky from school, and some friends ditched him to hang out with the more popular children who hung out at the arcades or movies, and whenever this happened to Rosie, many days he was left alone. To occupy his time, Rosie would sit inside a courtroom alongside a family, pretending to belong to that family, and listen to cases being held, just to see who the judge was and if he knew the people who were there to see the judge. While doing this Rosie learned a lot about the court system, such as the meaning of the words plea, allegations, continuance, and one of his favorites, cross-examine. Rosie took what he saw in the courtroom and used it in his everyday life, so when he became engaged in a discussion, it was always intense.

For example, in the fifth grade, Rosie's teacher requested that the class raise their hand to answer questions, because Rosie was not answering questions or raising his hand. The teacher called him to come up to the chalkboard, but Rosie did not want to because he had not raised his hand.

So Rosie asked his teacher why she would call on him, and she responded, "Because I wanted to."

Rosie's rebuttal back to her was "No, you said to raise your hand, and my hand was not raised."

The teacher responded, "Don't talk back to me."

He responded, "I'm not being disrespectful; I am just repeating what you said to the class."

The teacher replied, "Are you going to the board or to the office?" Rosie responded, "You are going to send me to the office because I did as you requested, and I have the class as a witness."

The teacher was fuming at this point, and she marched his little tail directly to the office. Rosie pleaded his case to the principal, but this lady was not trying to hear anything he had to say, so the principal suspended him. When Rosie arrived home, he then had to face his mother airing him out once again. He tried to plead his case with his mother, but she was not hearing him either. The teacher chose to make an example out of Rosie to the other students, that she did not play games and was not going to play games. She took the opportunity to show that she was somebody and that Rosie was nobody.

See how the equation *Nobody* + Opportunity = Somebody applies?

Rosie had brothers and sisters but still had a lot to do around the home. His oldest sister had a lot of records that he always played with as he got older. The more in depth he got with music, he began to stray away from his so-called friends. Not to mention as he aged, he saw a lot of those friends had gone astray by hanging out with the wrong crowd. At thirteen years old, many of the children were hustling and selling drugs with the money they made. The children bought clothing and scooters for themselves, which enticed Rosie to hustle as well but in a different manner. He got a summer job in which he was placed to work in the projects he lived in, cleaning the "pissy" staircases, raking leaves, and sweeping glass from broken bottles that everyone threw onto the grounds. The so-called friends and other people from the neighborhood picked on him because they knew him, and they knew the amount of money he made. This was embarrassing to Rosie, but he continued to work, and he took the monies from his laboring and bought school clothes and DJ equipment.

Rosie purchased DJ equipment because he wanted to learn how to deejay; plus, where he was cleaning up, a lot of older guys gave block parties, and that fascinated him. So Rosie bought some cheap equipment, but he needed to find someone to help him hook up the equipment. Once he got the equipment hooked up, he practiced in the house until he was ready to deejay a party for the city to hear him. A girl who Rosie was big on had a birthday coming up, and he asked her if she had found a DJ for her party. The girl did not have a DJ, so she gave Rosie the chance to deejay her party, although she was not big on Rosie. Rosie was still excited to be deejaying the party in the local recreation center, where everyone would have the chance to hear him play. Plus, he felt that if he did the party, it would be simple and guarantee him the girl who he liked, and that is why he opted to do the party for her—and for free.

Now remember, Rosie was new to learning how to hook up his equipment, so he had to write down everything. Unfortunately, Rosie encountered a problem with the speakers he was using because they were house speakers. He also did not have enough music, and because of the house speakers, his music could not be heard. This made Rosie very unhappy, and the girl was unhappy, and all the kids were laughing and talking about him. The girl then asked another boy who she knew liked her if his brother could finish deejaying her party. Of course, he said yes and reached out to his brother, and the kid said to Rosie, "Yo, get your toys out of here!" Rosie was so embarrassed.

The equation: *Nobody* + Opportunity = Somebody.

Going to school proved to be more difficult for Rosie as he got older. So, he started to leave the projects, and once he entered as a high school freshman, Rosie got a job at Burger King. But the kids in the projects still picked on him and made fun of him. Kids can be so cruel.

Every time the kids saw him with his uniform on, the kids would holler, "Rosie, give me a whopper with cheese and hold the onions."

No matter what, Rosie stayed focused because he wanted new equipment. Working at Burger King afforded Rosie better friends, and he began to build close relationships with them. Jerry, one of the friends who worked with Rosie, was white and lived in a nice neighborhood and invited Rosie to a pool party. Again, Rosie asked, "Do you have a DJ?" Jerry told him that he did not have a DJ, so Rosie volunteered himself as his DJ for his upcoming party, which was two months away. This was great because it would allow Rosie to get better prepared for the party. Rosie continued to work and save his money by sacrificing and by walking to and from Burger King rather than catching a bus, so he could purchase better equipment for the upcoming party of his new friend, Jerry.

While walking to work, Rosie came across a familiar face of a brother (a term Jersey folks recognize as another black man) named Spam who worked at the courthouse that he visited quite frequently in his younger days. Rosie tapped his window and asked him for a ride in trade for some free Burger King food. They chopped it up for a minute and Spam asked Rosie, "What are you planning to do with all those Burger King checks? Buy a car?"

Rosie replied quickly, "No, I'm buying DJ equipment." Spam then asked Rosie if he was a DJ.

Rosie replied, "Sort of."

Spam responded, "Are you a DJ? Yes or no."

Rosie told Spam that he was trying to become a DJ, and to his surprise he learned that Spam was a DJ for a club in the city. Rosie and Spam chopped it up a few more moments and then Rosie asked Spam if he could help him. Spam inquired about what Rosie needed help with, and Rosie informed him that he needed help with everything because he had no idea what to buy or how to properly hook up the equipment.

The plea: a familiar term Rosie had learned from visiting the courts. It was Rosie's plea to Spam for help. So Spam agreed if Rosie bought him some cuts, and the deal was made. Rosie asked if he could sit in on one of Spam's parties, but Spam warned him, "You are pushing it, kid." Rosie informed Spam of the party that he had booked coming up in two months and that he needed to prepare, so Spam gave him the go to meet him at the club by 7:00 p.m., and he would let him in through the back door.

Now the equation: *Nobody* + Opportunity = Somebody.

A lie is a lie and is wrong. Lawyers are good at it. The defense withholds the truth in this case to win and get their verdict. They prepare the witness on the stand to say what they want to say. So Rosie prepped Jerry on what to say when his mother called him. Rosie had told his mother that he was spending the night at Jerry's house, and she called Jerry, who verified the lie. Then Rosie went to 54th at 7:00 p.m., as instructed by Spam, but the club was not opening until 8:00 p.m. By 10:00 p.m., Rosie had written all the cuts (records) down and observed how the club was rocking, and he was so gassed up after seeing this. Rosie could not wait for Spam to go with him to shop for DJ equipment. Rosie had saved all that he could, and he came heavy with the dough. The two of them went shopping, and Spam showed him all he needed to get for starters, and Rosie bought records. Rosie also bought the same records that he had heard Spam play at the club the night before.

After they finished, Spam showed him how to hook up his equipment, and Rosie practiced and practiced. He did the same set he saw Spam do, so he was ready.

Now the equation: *Nobody* + Opportunity = Somebody. Rosie knew he needed support, which he learned in the courtroom. The defense will paint a picture to make you believe that their client is innocent. So Rosie asked Jerry if he could bring five friends: two girls and three boys. Jerry agreed, and this made Rosie very happy. This would be Rosie's first time at a nightclub on his own, and he fell in love with it. The girls he invited were popular, and so by inviting them, he would get the word out to others whether he was a bad DJ or a good DJ. By getting the word out that he was good would mean that all the people in the projects would know as well. That is free PR (public relations); he knew that from court, as well as work labor laws. So the day of the party, the three guys, the muscle, and those kids were amazed they never left the projects, so they were shocked that he got them like Spam said and started his set. Rosie was just like Spam; you would swear it was him with the mixed crowd, and they loved him. The older people loved him as well. Jerry's father was about to pay him, but Rosie said, "No, you good, sir."

NOBODY

Now the equation: *Nobody* + Opportunity = Somebody. Rosie watched and did everything the same as Spam did in the club. Jerry's father was so pleased and impressed with Rosie, he asked Rosie, "What is it that you want if you will not take money?" Rosie knew Jerry's father was a dean at a catholic school.

So Rosie asked him for a referral to all the schools that he was in connection with. Mr. Sandler said that he would be happy to oblige that request—the art of negotiating, which he learned in property court. Anyhow, the five friends who he invited to the party did exactly what Rosie thought they would do, which was spread the "talk." Those kids told everybody in the projects and in the school, and that made Rosie happy.

Do the math. Mr. Sadler contacted Rosie and asked him if he would be willing to DJ a Sadie Hawkins dance for his school, and Rosie happily obliged. But what exactly was a Sadie Hawkins dance? Mr. Sandler just laughed, and he hired Rosie for the Sadie Hawkins event, and the people loved him after doing that one free party. His work got him lined up for a contract for twelve school prom and junior prom events, along with high school parties and skating rinks. Those kids told everybody Rosie was getting a lot of money for the pool party, but they did not know that he had done the party for free. Rosie gave them twenty dollars for helping to spread the word. Rosie learned in the courtroom that the defense dressed up their witnesses and prepped them as well, such as he had done.

Again, what is the question?

With all the money from the parties that Rosie was doing, he was able to buy himself a car. This allowed Rosie to really be able to travel, and he drove during his last two years of high school. In his senior year, he had to write a paper on what he wanted to be when he got out of school. Rosie knew then what it was he wanted to become: to have a major record company. In those days Rosie could rap and DJ. By midterm, Rosie had enrolled in the Center for Media Arts.

Rosie knew he had to advance his skill, so when he graduated, he would be ready for the next level. When you have goals and dreams, you must remain focused and not get distracted.

Rosie was full of himself and became a teenage dad. This was a devastation for Rosie because he did not know anything about being a father. The girl and Rosie were not even together, and she gave Rosie the "blues." The baby boy was born in April, and Rosie graduated in June, and then it went sour. Rosie's son's mother thought Rosie was a big-time DJ, so she took him to court. Rosie bought clothes and paid for the baby shower after he graduated. However, money slowed down because he did not have proms or school events. So Rosie was seventeen years old and now in court for real this time. Rosie asked the case worker if he could see the judge by himself, and she told him that he could not see the judge because this was a judgment order—in other words, Rosie was in trouble.

The judgment hearing ruled for Rosie, a nobody, to pay a high child support order like he was somebody important. Rosie had no gigs lined up, which made him fall behind on his child support order. This also created difficulty with getting back into school because with a back-child support order against him, Rosie was not able to enroll at the Center for Media Arts because he owed child support. This shattered Rosie, but he did not give up. He went back to the courts to request an adjustment or modification to the order. The courts asked him if he was serious and informed him that he had only one month to settle arrears.

Rosie got a job, and he received his first paycheck, but when he opened the check, it read "void." He had worked so hard and did not even receive thirty cents. The government took the whole check. Rosie was so mad, and he quit the job. He said he could not work for free. The girl was trying to destroy him, and she was not trying to help him. So his ego kicked in and made matters worse. The order got bigger, and the interest piled on.

Rosie received mail to appear in court, but Rosie went out of town to see a girl instead, which led to a bench warrant. He learned in the courtroom a missed appearance would cause a warrant for your arrest. He did not truly believe that they would come and get him, especially with other criminal activities going on in the world.

It was a hot day in July, on a Saturday, that a gray moving van rode through the projects. Rosie always kept a folding chair in his trunk and sat in the middle of the street like he was out at the beach. The van blocked Rosie, a nobody, and then the boys with the warrant jumped out of the van and made the arrest. They had the opportunity to stick it to Rosie, like he was somebody.

Rosie got locked up on Saturday, and he knew he was not going to make bail, so he had to wait to see the judge on Tuesday. Tuesday came, and he saw the same judge after lunch, and Rosie waived his rights to have a public defender. And by doing that, the judge would have to reschedule. The judge was a woman, and he felt that she wanted him to suffer. The judge asked Rosie if he could make bail, and he informed her that he was not able to make bail and would be representing himself in the case. The judge nodded her head and then explained to him that for sentencing purposes he would be required to have an attorney. Rosie assured her that he understood, and so the judge proceeded. The judge asked if he had a vehicle, and Rosie responded that he did not have a car. The judge showed Rosie pictures of a vehicle with the registration under his name.

At this point, the judge was now mad, and she put him on the docket for her calendar, early the following week. Then she sounded to Rosie, "When you come back to see me, be sure to bring your toothbrush."

What is the question?

Rosie went home and talked to his mother, who was so lost and mad. The day came for him to come back to court, and they appointed him a public defender. The judge read the charges and sentenced him to three months. Rosie did three months and could not believe it. When he came home, he had to get on the ball. Rosie had to think of a way to make money; if he worked, the court would take it all.

So Rosie went to the club, and after the club he stopped at White Castle, which was packed with people. There was a guy in the parking lot playing music. Everybody was around his car—the majority were women—so Rosie asked the brother what it was that he was playing. The guy responded, "Young buck, you don't know nothing about this music."

Rosie said, "You right, and that is why I am asking." He told Rosie that it was deep soul, and Rosie inquired where he could find it. The guy told him to turn his dial to 1430 WNJR. Rosie hurried to grab his food and jumped into his car to turn his radio to the station, but he could not find the station, so he yelled back to the guy that he could not find it. Then the guy told him to turn the radio dial to the 1430 AM dial. He did it and wrote down the information of the station.

Rosie went to the station in downtown Newark and spoke to the program director and asked him for a job. The director said that they were not hiring. Rosie said he would volunteer because he could not get paid anyway.

Rosie wanted to learn the music and needed the music anyways, so working for free was no problem. He desired the knowledge. Once given the opportunity, Rosie devoted his time to the radio station and started to learn the music and collected the music they gave him.

So Rosie went back to that White Castle and asked the manager if he would allow Rosie to set up a table and a radio in the corner to sell tapes, and in return he would give the manager $100. The manager asked Rosie what would happen if he did not make sales. Rosie told him that would not be a problem, so the manager took him up on the offer to sell his music. Rosie sold his tapes for at least thirty minutes for five dollars each, and in sixty minutes for ten dollars each. He grabbed a breadbasket from the back of the store where he stocked his tapes.

On Friday nights around 10:00 p.m., he would set up in the corner of the store and play the tape that he had made. Once the customers heard the music upon entering the store, the customers would visit his table and buy his music. Rosie always sold out on Friday and Saturday nights, and he made enough money to buy a new car.

Do the math. Rosie named the tapes Quiet Hour. Rosie was still a nobody at this point, in his opinion, compared to the drug dealers. Being a dad was hard, and Rosie did enjoy it, but he did not enjoy the drama with the mother of his son. Rosie wanted more, and he grew tired of being in Jersey. Rosie met another woman on the West Coast, and he started hanging out there. When he came back to Jersey, he was able to re-enroll in the Center for Media Arts in New York. He knew he was going to do something special. Rosie went into Englewood, New Jersey, and applied for a regular job at the record company. He did a lot of work there but did not get paid.

He met a lot of artists while working there, and that made Rosie want to start a record company, because he had a child to support now. Rosie realized that he could not continue to work for free because he owed the courts. So Rosie went back home and started to play at a block party the next day. He went to school when he did lab work, and he did major rap group music for their record. Rosie went back west and got closer with this chick he had met out there.

The question. Seeing how a record company was run, Rosie knew right then he wanted to start a record company, but the decision he made to move out to the West Coast with no family took a toll on him and his relationship. The challenges proved to be overwhelming, even more so after getting married at a young age and then having to live with his churchgoing in-laws. It became tough to maintain the relationship, and he felt less than a man, but he continued to push himself and tried hard to do the right thing, living with people of the church. Not truly understanding church, nor the Bible, Rosie received harsh judgment from the in-laws every minute on everything. His wife, at the time, did not believe in him at all—and neither did her family.

One day, Rosie had a big argument with her in the park, and the police were called out to the scene. Rosie was arrested for domestic violence. Although Rosie did not touch her, he had to remain in jail until Tuesday—for nothing, in his mind. Rosie was so mad, and he thought, *Not again*. "I am back in jail for nothing, only this time for one month."

Rosie and his wife were at odds, and he tried to fix what happened. Rosie went to see the judge who then ordered him to pay a heavy fine and take classes that he had to pay for. This angered him because he was already on child support and was now ordered to give the courts more money for another case. And these supposedly godly folks did not try to help him but instead hurt him. The judge looked at him as a nobody; plus he felt that this gave her an opportunity to make an example out of him to become somebody.

Rosie went to the ordered classes and started to embrace it and learned a little something.

Unfortunately, as time went on, Rosie and the in-laws still did not see eye-to-eye. One day a big argument came about, and his wife's mother picked up a broom at him. Rosie responded to her threat by saying, "I hope you plan to sweep with that broom."

So when the father arrived, Rosie was ordered to leave their home, and if he did not leave, they would be calling the police out to the home. Rosie knew that was not an option, so he left but had nowhere to go. So he went to a local bus station and stayed there. Rosie slept on the bench at the bus station and washed up in the public restroom. Rosie never thought he would be in such a situation. Then one day, one of his homeboys saw him and asked him if he was all right. Although Rosie told his homeboy that he was okay, his homeboy knew that he was lying because he had never seen Rosie not looking fresh and looking like money. After seeing Rosie in his situation, Rosie's homeboy went back and spread the word to other friends that Rosie may be sleeping at the bus station.

They all got together and came down to the bus station and rescued Rosie and told him that he was coming to stay with them. His homeboy from Jersey who was living out there and did music took two of his mattresses and placed them on his floor and gave Rosie a bed to sleep on. Rosie cried himself to sleep that night because someone cared for him. The apartment was located down the road from a community college, so again Rosie started to get back on his mission for success.

Now what is the question?

Rosie went back to Jersey and to the school where he learned studio work, and he made a track to bring back to the West Coast. Before he left Jersey, he told some people what his plans were, and he would be back to shop his music. Rosie needed to make money, so he applied with this mobile DJ company that he had to audition for.

So you know what this meant for Rosie? Rosie chose different records for the audition, and he knew he was going to get hired—and he did. Rosie did that job well, and he did the sound for the city in the special events department. So Rosie took an early out on his job back in Jersey and opened a studio at the apartment. He bought all the equipment and let the guys make music and groomed them as well.

Rosie took up more classes at the college and paid for his license. Rosie knew what he wanted because Rosie paid for all his classes. However, he told the professor that he was not going to take any test or do any of the homework. He was simply in class to get the knowledge, and if he got a grade of F, that would not allow him to go to the next level. So he asked the professor to give him a D, not an F, because receiving an F would mean *free*. Since Rosie was at least paying for his own classes, he was not accepting an F.

The dean asked him, "What about a degree?"

Rosie informed him that he was never enrolling in school for that (a degree).

Rosie got all he asked for from the dean, and he had all access to the student theater. He was on his way. Rosie needed credit, so he made his own credits.

Rosie then went to a small bank with $500 and put it in a CD (certificate of deposit; where you deposit your own money and gain interest). Rosie went to another small bank and did the same thing, and then he went back to the first bank and took out a $500 loan and then another $550 loan from the second bank. He paid them both off by flip-flopping and paying the debts. He was able to obtain a line of credit from both banks.

Rosie moved out and had a real record company. Rosie did payroll and production, so he had to change it up. His license had three companies under one umbrella: a management company, a production company, and a record company. Rosie was totally independent, and he cut the cost on everything. He had three nightclubs so his artists could perform and throw after parties at one of the nightclubs. Rosie got another license, which was a class-one promoter, and with this license he would be able to promote concerts. Rosie rented the San Diego and the Thomas & Mack Center in Vegas where he put on some big concerts because he now controlled everything.

Now ask the question.

So Rosie sent money orders back to the courts in Jersey, and he vowed to himself that he would not ever get in the rears with child support again. Rosie knew he had to spend his own money to have control and support for his dream, and then the divorce came. The heifer, referred to as the ex-wife, tried to take everything that he had worked for. However, she could not take everything because he did not have full ownership in his name, so she was not able to get the studio or the clubs. He put the guys' names on the track he made.

When he first moved out there, he worked at the radio station for free, so he did a show and built a strong relationship by doing that, and he got his very own song played. Having a hit record is hard when you are funding it. Rosie put the guys on the road and set up a promo tour. The first show was in Los Angeles at the Hollywood Palladium nightclub for the ASCAP conference, and Rosie spent more money for the music conference than what he would have paid for a home in cash. He took a big hit with the divorce and not seeing the results of his labor, and with all the flying back and forth, he had so many miles from flying.

As Rosie drove past Micky D's, he got the idea of the fifty-fifty deal. He was tired of asking, so he wrote a proposal, bought a ticket to Chicago, and met with the marketing director for McDonalds. Rosie's office was like a library filled with a myriad of research—just as he had learned in the courtroom process of what the lawyers do to prepare for their case.

Now what is the question?

What does McDonalds have to do with music? Okay, allow me to break it down. McDonald's has a university in which they sell in one store a million dollars in coffee. Rosie knew they had a kid's meal, but they did not have a teenager's meal. So Rosie proposed to Micky's D's that the MM meals stand for McDonald's music meal. Rosie put a three-song CD in the meal, which McDonald's would create, and Rosie would receive one dollar and Micky D's would keep the rest. By doing that before the Internet existed, he would have sold more music than any record company in history with one dollar in six months. He would have been a billionaire, and the artist would have been in one year as well. Now, Rosie asked for one dollar on every meal sold, and here is the breakdown.

Rosie proposed to Brian, the marketing director and project manager, and a young guy named Shawn who was an assistant for special projects that he only requires. His proposal was that Ronald McDonald House Charities gets twenty-five cents for each meal sold, and like Rosie said he would make a thirty-second commercial for the product. All Rosie needed was for them to air the commercial.

Such a fifty-fifty deal that he proposed was better than a deal with a major record company would have been. However, if you just started your own deal, then it would be an eighty-twenty P & D deal (pressing and distribution) with a major record company. So that would put Rosie in the position to give his artist a 360 deal to make money for his company. For those who do not know what 360 means, it is when the record company participates in all aspects of the artist's career, like touring and merchandising. For every move the artist made, Rosie would get paid. If the artist sells $500,000, the artist would get $250,000, the label will take 15 percent from that artist, and it can be whatever the pay is. It could be three cents a record or one cent, or even a dime. Rosie changed the theory by giving McDonald's four dollars, and he would still control payroll for his company. The worst he could have done was accept fifty cents and still be on top. Brian loved the pitch but Shawn did not, and Rosie felt that Shawn just did not have logical reasoning. To get a famous artist would cost them more and lose more control. The deal had to be made with both Brian and Shawn being on board, so they knocked it down.

That hurt Rosie bad, and he had something to prove, but he was failing. He spoke to his ex-wife, and deep down he still cared for her. He began to ponder over his life, failing as a husband and as a businessman. All Rosie wanted to do was to succeed in life and have his record company.

So he started attending church and reading the Bible, praying, fasting, and practicing celibacy until he decided to marry again. Reading the book of knowledge, Rosie learned two important scriptures: "You have not because you ask not" (James 4:2–3); and "If you believe, you will receive whatever you ask in prayer" (Mark 11:24). He was angry that he accepted and he did not get what he asked for.

His ex-wife looked at him as a lowlife. He had lost his car. Rosie's life had gotten bad, and as he reflected on his life, depression sank in and got the best of him. Rosie booked a red-eye flight back to Jersey and bought himself some high-strength sleeping pills and M&M's candies. He went home to pack and switched out the candies for sleeping pills. The day of his flight, he took his window seat in coach class, all the way in the back and next to the lavatory, flying from the West Coast back to the East Coast.

After being in the air for an hour and a half of his three-hour flight time, Rosie tried swallowing the bag of pills. Rosie's plan was to take all the pills before the plane landed, so someone would find him in his eternal peace, but something in his gut would not allow him to finish out the plan. It was the pain that he would have caused his mother, and Rosie felt that no mother deserved that pain, especially his mother. He landed in Jersey and went directly to visit his mother and friends. He talked to his mother about moving back home because he was not doing well out there, and she responded, "You always have a home here." Rosie tried to keep himself busy by working, but his heart was not in Jersey anymore. He maintained contact with his friends back in the Bay and in LA. The publicist Rosie hired called and told him about a pitch that Rosie had worked on with this lady in the past, so he emailed her his output on the idea.

Rosie stayed on the course by trying to make something out of nothing. Even with his challenges and his child support issues, however, he loved spending time with his son. He got a job, but on the first day of working the job, he realized he hated the job and quit. Rosie always said that if he could not take care of himself, then he could not take care of anybody else. So he withdrew the rest of his money and gave it to his son's mother and told her that he was leaving.

Rosie prepared and moved back to the West Coast and went back to the basics. He went to all the hotels and made a bid to do all the weddings with the event planners and asked them if they could include his services into their packages. Upon arriving back to Las Vegas, he applied at a mobile DJ company. An older white man who was known as a racist did not hire him, so he decided to go independent. Rosie did not have a job, but he created a job. Rosie had six casinos to give him their accounts to do all their weddings, and he was back in action. He got a call from the publicist in

Los Angeles, and MTV accepted the show that was pitched. He enrolled in Disney Writers Pilot, the first time he wrote for one of their television shows.

So what is the question?

ABC called Rosie and sent him the application; however, Rosie did not know what to write on the application. He picked his favorite show and wrote an episode, and luckily it got picked up. The pay was decent, but he got no exclusives, and this meant that it was free material. He never told anyone because they would not believe it until this day. Rosie loves the show. Rosie had to make decisions when he was running his record company. He shot videos and did a lot of film permits, casting crew, and got it played on BET.

For $5,000 for one spin and Rosie did everything majors were doing with little money. A well-known CEO came to Rosie's house to offer a proposition with his company, and Rosie was tempted but did not take it.

Rosie was single for ten years after his divorce and a father to a child back in Jersey. He had met women all over, but he did not get serious because of his focus. Remaining focused motivated Rosie's ambitions, and then another episode popped up in his life. His son was not doing well back home in Jersey, so the mother called Rosie to ask if their son could come and live with him.

Rosie gave it the okay. He was in no position to have a kid full-time, and he did not even have a decent place. But Rosie wasn't going to let his son be a nobody, so what he did was sell all of his studio equipment, get a two-bedroom apartment, and pay for insurance so that his son would be able to participate in sports. Rosie fell back and put his dream on hold. Rosie wanted his son to have a decent life, and that is what he did.

Amazed at himself for making the decision to give up his dream to raise his son, Rosie picked up three part-time jobs and continued to DJ to make the household lifestyle comfortable. His son was better and had a vision with him. His son was afforded the opportunity to go back home to Jersey every weekend, until one day he told his mom that he was not going back to live with Rosie. This hurt Rosie badly because he had enrolled him into football camps, and Rosie had given up everything for his son. And for him not to care and say that he was not coming back destroyed Rosie. Rosie felt that he had let everyone down who looked up to him, but people told him that he had not let them down; however he saw it differently. While all of this was happening, Rosie decided to go home for Thanksgiving to relax and enjoy dinner with his mom and brother.

After a week, Rosie left Jersey and returned to Vegas where he worked and kept himself busy to find himself. Then he received a phone call from his sister on Christmas Eve—his mother was in the hospital. Rosie immediately booked a flight back to Jersey, and once on the flight, Rosie cried. He cried for the first time over so much, and he began to reflect on the first funeral he ever went to. He was nine years old, and his two friends knocked on the door on a Saturday morning to ask if Rosie could come outside. He told them that he was not able to come out to play on that day because he had to go shopping.

They said, "cool" and to get with them once he returned from shopping. Unfortunately, when he got back home, the police and ambulance were all over the place, and there was a white van in front of the apartment building. He asked what was happening and was informed that one of the kids who had come to get Rosie to play earlier that day was killed on the elevator. Rosie never imagined going on a class field trip that was to a funeral. Rosie landed and dashed right over to the hospital and visited with his mother and had their last words. Rosie was alone now, with no companionship. It was at that moment he said to himself, "It is time to make some changes."

Rosie struggled for a while, with no studio, and the goal of a major record company was gone. He felt defeated, but Rosie made a switch and said that he was leaving the West Coast and decided to head south to be closer to family. Rosie moved and caught hell when he came south. There was no southern hospitality. He worked in a grocery store, and he was not happy. Then he got another job that he liked, and Rosie started to travel and put his DJ skills to use. The first gig he did was at this club on this major street. The crowd booed Rosie, and the owner refused to pay him. It was at this moment that Rosie promised himself to never do any more low-budget stuff at this place.

Rosie started to meet people and made a pitch to venues. One venue set up a meeting and hired Rosie for a three-day event. Rosie felt a way that he had never felt from working at a smoothie shop.

Questions, please.

Rosie's partner from upstate meant everything to him, and the chemistry and words were everything. Knowing you can get pushed when you are down. Rosie did the three-day event, and he killed it, as expected. The venue and Rosie signed a contract, and his partner from upstate helped him. Rosie bought his first house and realized he came a long way, and still now Rosie is on the grind and hustling. He continued to write and dream. He started to go after what he really wanted to accomplish. The first thing was to put God first, and he made a real strong effort to have a relationship with God and understand his word and try to live by his word.

The contract was doing well, and Rosie was enjoying it. He also had his eyes on a bigger "fish to fry," which Rosie always dreamed of bigger and that was to help others and be a blessing for someone else. He was not focused on the big payday but on being the light to help that *nobody* with an opportunity to be somebody. Rosie got an email from the person and the company he wanted to work with, saying that he was invited to a virtual meeting on a Thursday. He was prepared, and it could not have been ten minutes before he was saying "thank you" for all God had done for him because he knew that this was not possible without his help. The meeting came and Rosie's computer was down because of a big storm that night, so he had to log on again, and he finally got through. Rosie met with one of his representatives and blew him away.

He asked Rosie when he could come to London, and Rosie replied, "Tonight." They laughed, and the representative told him that he would work out well with their company. Rosie went into his room and dropped to his knees and cried and said, "Thank you, Lord, because you surely did not have to bless me, and I promise to be a blessing to others!"

Acknowledgments

The Special Page

This page is dedicated to special people who did special things at special times in my life.

With God, I learned that things are possible through him and with him. I am nothing, and I *thank* him with all my heart (Philippians 4:13).

10-22-32: Blessed me with the mind and life to become the man that I am.

02-24-24: Thank you for bringing me into the world and showing me vision.

10-14-64: Helped me out from day one to get back financially, so I could acquire things, and for that I am forever grateful.

05-22-48: Blessed me with the ears to listen and the lips to talk. Our endless conversations and planning. I will always miss.

10-23-36: Blessed me with the word "proud," and that meant a lot.

12-08-58: Blessed me by allowing me to never allow someone to look down on me. Always there to help me, even knowing that I feared 12-08-58.

05-05-42: Never said "no" at any time, and it was always an open-door policy and love.

07-13-69: Always being there through my travels of seeing my bad and my good on the views we shared and experiences that were incredible.

09-08-69: We have always had a strong history for each other from buying the first car and starting the first business.

02-10-76: Blessed me with the hands that helped to put this masterpiece together, and thank you for the myriad of great conversations that helped me to grow spiritually, as well as personally.

03-11-76: Helped me in ways that I cannot pay back from having nothing and not accepting anything. A true blessing, and I will always be grateful!

07-16-70: Blessed me with a chance and understanding. You gave me the confidence and paved a journey that I do not want to ever end.

12-12-51: Thank you. You have always been someone I looked up to. 10-24-57: You blessed me with the vision to see and what not to be.

04-29-67: Thank you for blessing me with the ride of hip-hop records and tapes.

06-05-72: Thank you for being a pain since day one.

CPSIA information can be obtained
at www.ICGtesting.com
Printed in the USA
BVHW042221211220
596220BV00004B/13